THE KETO EGG FAST DIET

COOKBOOK FOR WOMEN

Simple Healthy Egg-Centric Meals to Boost Your Keto Journey

Anita F.MS, RDN. McCluskey

"Disclaimer:

The recipes and information in "*The Keto Egg Fast Diet Cookbook for Women*" are intended for educational and informational purposes only. This content should not be considered a substitute for professional medical advice, diagnosis, or treatment. Always consult your physician or a qualified health provider with any questions related to medical conditions. The author and publisher of this cookbook disclaim any liability for adverse effects or consequences arising from the use of the information or recipes provided.

Dedication

To every amazing woman dedicated to enhancing her health and well-being through the power of nutrition. May this book be your guide and source of inspiration on your keto journey. You are more powerful, resilient, and capable than you realize. This is for you.

Contents

Chapter 8: Troubleshooting and Tips
- Common Challenges on the Egg Fast
- How to Break a Weight Loss Plateau
- Managing Cravings and Staying on Track
- Frequently Asked Questions

Chapter 9: Maintaining Your Results
- Reintroducing Foods After the Egg Fast
- Building a Sustainable Keto Lifestyle
- Continuing Your Weight Loss Journey
- Healthy Habits for Long-Term Success

Bonus Chapter: 7-Day Keto-Friendly Exercise Plan for Women

Conclusion
- Celebrating Your Success
- Staying Committed to Your Health Goals
- Final Words of Encouragement
- Tips for Long-Term Success

Introduction

Welcome to *"The Keto Egg Fast Diet Cookbook for Women: Simple Healthy Egg-Centric Meals to Boost Your Keto Journey"*. Whether you're new to keto or looking for a way to break through a stubborn weight loss plateau, you've made a great decision to focus on your health and well-being.

As women, we often juggle multiple responsibilities—whether it's work, family, or social commitments—while trying to maintain our health and fitness. This can feel like a lot to manage, especially when it comes to making healthy food choices. But you don't have to do it alone. This book is here to support you, offering not just recipes but a practical and manageable approach to the Keto Egg Fast, tailored specifically for women.

The Keto Egg Fast is a tool that helps reset your body, break through plateaus, and kickstart your weight loss journey. It's about more than just shedding pounds; it's about feeling energized, empowered, and in control of your health. By focusing on simple, nutrient-dense ingredients—primarily eggs, healthy fats, and a bit of cheese—this diet provides your body with the necessary fuel to burn fat effectively, while keeping you satisfied and energized.

This book will guide you step by step through the Keto Egg Fast, from understanding the science behind it to getting your kitchen ready with the essentials. You'll find easy-to-follow recipes that are quick to prepare, making it simpler to stay on track, even on your busiest days. We've also included meal plans and tips to help you succeed, whether you're doing the Egg Fast for just a few days or planning to extend it.

Most importantly, this book is about you. It's about giving you the tools and knowledge you need to make lasting changes. The Keto Egg Fast is more than just a diet; it's a way to take control of your health, feel good in your body, and embrace a lifestyle that supports your goals.

Every journey begins with a single step, and you've already taken that step by picking up this book. Let's walk this path together, one delicious egg-based meal at a time.

Chapter 1

Getting Started with the Keto Egg Fast

Understanding the Basics: How the Egg Fast Works

The Keto Egg Fast is a short-term, low-carb, high-fat diet designed to help you enter or deepen ketosis—a metabolic state where your body burns fat for energy instead of carbohydrates. For many women, this diet serves as a powerful reset, allowing the body to overcome weight loss plateaus and restart progress on the keto journey.

At its core, the Egg Fast is simple: it involves consuming eggs, butter, and cheese for a specific number of days, usually between 3 to 5. These foods are chosen for their balanced mix of fats, proteins, and essential nutrients while keeping carbohydrate intake minimal. This combination supports your body in maintaining ketosis, optimizing fat burning.

Rules and Guidelines for a Successful Egg Fast

While the Egg Fast is straightforward, there are some key guidelines to follow to ensure success:

1. **Eat at least six eggs daily:** Eggs are your primary source of protein and nutrients during the fast. Aim for at least six eggs each day to meet your nutritional needs.

2. **Include a tablespoon of fat with each egg:** Pair each egg with a tablespoon of healthy fat, such as butter, coconut oil, or olive oil. This will help keep you full and provide the fats necessary to support ketosis.

3. **Incorporate a small amount of cheese:** You can have up to 1 ounce of cheese per

egg. Cheese adds flavor and variety while contributing additional fat and protein.

4. **Space meals evenly throughout the day:** Try to eat every 3 to 5 hours, even if you're not particularly hungry. This helps maintain steady energy levels and prevents overeating later.

5. **Stay hydrated:** Drink plenty of water throughout the day. You can also have unsweetened tea, black coffee, or bone broth. Electrolyte supplements are also helpful in preventing imbalances during the fast.

6. **Stick to the plan for 3 to 5 days:** The Egg Fast is intended to be short-term. Most women find that 3 to 5 days is sufficient to break a plateau or jumpstart weight loss. After this period, transition back to a regular keto diet gradually.

Preparing Your Kitchen

Essential Tools and Ingredients

To make your Egg Fast as smooth as possible, it's essential to prepare your kitchen with the right tools and ingredients. Here's what you'll need:

- **High-Quality Eggs:** Organic, pasture-raised eggs are ideal for their superior nutrition and flavor. Stock up on enough eggs to last through your fast.

- **Healthy Fats:** Butter, ghee, coconut oil, and olive oil are all excellent choices. Keep these on hand for cooking and meal prep.

- **Cheese:** Choose high-quality, full-fat cheeses like cheddar, mozzarella, or cream cheese. Shredded cheese is also a convenient option for quick meals.

- **Basic Cooking Tools:** Make sure you have a good non-stick frying pan, mixing bowls, spatulas, and measuring cups. An egg cooker or poacher can also be useful for quick meal prep.

- **Seasonings and Spices:** While the Egg Fast is simple, you can still enjoy a variety of flavors. Keep your favorite keto-friendly seasonings and spices on hand to add variety to your meals.

By understanding the basics and following these guidelines, you're setting yourself up for success. The Keto Egg Fast may be challenging, but with the right preparation and mindset, it can be a rewarding experience that propels you toward your health and weight loss goals. Now, let's dive into the upcoming chapters, where you'll find a variety of delicious and satisfying recipes to keep you motivated and on track throughout your Egg Fast journey.

Chapter 2

Energizing Breakfast Recipes

A nutritious, keto-friendly breakfast is the foundation for maintaining energy, focus, and reducing cravings throughout the day. The Keto Egg Fast focuses on simple yet delicious egg-based meals, and breakfast is the perfect time to get creative while sticking to the plan. The recipes in this chapter are designed to be quick, satisfying, and packed with the essential nutrients needed to start your day strong.

Whether you're on a tight schedule or enjoying a slower morning, these breakfast recipes will help you feel energized and committed to your keto journey. They are rich in healthy fats and protein, designed to keep you full and satisfied until your next meal. Remember, starting your day on the right note is crucial for long-term success. Let's dive into these flavorful, egg-centric breakfasts!

Classic Butter Scrambled Eggs

Kick off your day with these rich and creamy butter scrambled eggs. This simple, yet satisfying dish perfectly embodies the Keto Egg Fast's high-fat, low-carb philosophy, ensuring a delicious start to your morning.

Ingredients:
- 3 large eggs
- 2 tablespoons unsalted butter
- Salt and pepper to taste

Instructions:
1. Beat the eggs in a bowl until fully combined.
2. Heat the butter in a non-stick pan over medium-low heat.
3. Add the eggs to the pan, stirring continuously until they are soft and creamy.
4. Season with salt and pepper before serving.

Storage:
These scrambled eggs are best enjoyed fresh, but can be kept in an airtight container in the fridge for up

to 2 days. Reheat them gently on the stovetop to avoid overcooking.

Nutritional Information (Per Serving):
- Calories: 270
- Fat: 24g
- Protein: 12g
- Carbohydrates: 1g

Fluffy Cheese Omelette

This fluffy cheese omelette is a great way to add variety to your breakfast routine. Combining eggs and cheese, it offers a satisfying balance of protein and fat, keeping you full throughout the morning.

Ingredients:
- 3 large eggs
- 1 ounce shredded cheddar cheese
- 1 tablespoon butter
- Salt and pepper to taste

Instructions:
1. Whisk the eggs until light and frothy.

2. Melt the butter in a non-stick skillet over medium heat.

3. Pour in the eggs and cook without stirring until the edges begin to set.

4. Sprinkle cheese over half of the omelette, fold it in half, and cook for another minute until the cheese is melted and the eggs are fully cooked.

5. Season with salt and pepper to taste.

Storage:

Store in an airtight container in the fridge for up to 2 days. Reheat in a non-stick skillet over low heat.

Nutritional Information (Per Serving):

- Calories: 320
- Fat: 27g
- Protein: 18g
- Carbohydrates: 1g

Spinach and Mushroom Egg Muffins

These spinach and mushroom egg muffins are perfect for a quick, on-the-go breakfast. Nutritious and flavorful, they're easy to prepare ahead of time, making your Keto Egg Fast convenient and delicious.

Ingredients:
- 6 large eggs
- 1/2 cup spinach, chopped
- 1/2 cup mushrooms, diced
- 1/4 cup shredded cheese (optional)
- 2 tablespoons butter, melted
- Salt and pepper to taste

Instructions:
1. Preheat the oven to 350°F (175°C) and grease a muffin tin with butter.
2. In a large bowl, whisk the eggs, then stir in the spinach, mushrooms, and cheese.
3. Pour the mixture into the muffin tin, filling each cup about three-quarters full.
4. Bake for 15-20 minutes or until the muffins are fully set.
5. Let them cool slightly before removing them from the tin.

Storage:
Store in an airtight container in the fridge for up to 5 days, or freeze for up to 1 month. Reheat in the microwave or oven before serving.

Nutritional Information (Per Serving):
- Calories: 140
- Fat: 10g
- Protein: 10g
- Carbohydrates: 2g

Bacon-Wrapped Egg Cups

These bacon-wrapped egg cups offer a protein-packed, flavorful breakfast that's bound to become a staple. The crispy bacon and soft egg make a delicious and indulgent combination.

Ingredients:
- 6 large eggs
- 6 slices of bacon
- Salt and pepper to taste

Instructions:

1. Preheat the oven to 375°F (190°C) and grease a muffin tin.

2. Cook the bacon slices in a skillet until they start to crisp but are still flexible.

3. Line each muffin cup with a slice of bacon, forming a ring.

4. Crack an egg into each bacon-lined cup, season with salt and pepper.

5. Bake for 12-15 minutes, or until the eggs are cooked to your preference.

Storage:

Store in an airtight container in the fridge for up to 3 days. Reheat in the oven for the best texture.

Nutritional Information (Per Serving):

- Calories: 200
- Fat: 15g
- Protein: 14g
- Carbohydrates: 1g

Egg and Cheese Chaffles

Chaffles, or cheese waffles, are a popular keto choice. This egg-centric version is simple and satisfying, making it perfect for your Egg Fast. Enjoy them as a quick breakfast or snack.

Ingredients:
- 2 large eggs
- 1 cup shredded mozzarella cheese

Instructions:
1. Preheat your waffle maker.
2. In a bowl, whisk together the eggs and cheese.
3. Pour the mixture into the waffle maker and cook until golden brown and crispy, following the manufacturer's instructions.
4. Serve immediately, or store for later.

Storage:
Store chaffles in an airtight container in the fridge for up to 3 days, or freeze for up to 1 month. Reheat in a toaster.

<u>Nutritional Information (Per Serving)</u>:
- Calories: 320
- Fat: 24g
- Protein: 24g
- Carbohydrates: 2g

Keto Pancakes with Egg Base

These Keto Pancakes, made with an egg base, are light, fluffy, and delicious. They're a low-carb, high-protein way to start your day, especially when paired with sugar-free syrup or fresh berries.

<u>Ingredients</u>:
- 3 large eggs
- 2 ounces cream cheese, softened
- 1/4 teaspoon vanilla extract
- 1/4 teaspoon baking powder
- Butter or oil for cooking

<u>Instructions</u>:
1. Blend the eggs, cream cheese, vanilla extract, and baking powder in a blender until smooth.
2. Heat a non-stick skillet over medium heat, adding a small amount of butter or oil.

3. Pour about 1/4 cup of the batter into the skillet for each pancake, cooking until bubbles form on the surface.
4. Flip and cook until golden brown.

Storage:
Store pancakes in an airtight container in the fridge for up to 3 days. They can also be frozen and reheated in a skillet or toaster.

Nutritional Information (Per Serving):
- Calories: 210
- Fat: 18g
- Protein: 10g
- Carbohydrates: 2g

Keto Egg Burrito with Avocado Salsa

This savory egg burrito pairs fluffy scrambled eggs with a fresh avocado salsa for a nutrient-packed breakfast. The combination of healthy fats and protein makes this a perfect way to fuel your body for the day ahead.

Ingredients
- 4 large eggs
- 1 tbsp butter
- ½ cup shredded cheddar cheese
- 1 small avocado, diced
- 1 tbsp lime juice
- 1 tbsp chopped cilantro
- Salt and pepper to taste

Procedure
1. In a small bowl, combine diced avocado, lime juice, cilantro, and salt to make the salsa.
2. Melt butter in a skillet and scramble the eggs to your preferred doneness. Season with salt and pepper.
3. Lay the scrambled eggs on a plate, sprinkle with cheese, and top with avocado salsa.
4. Roll up the eggs like a burrito and enjoy.

Brilliant Tip: You can add a touch of hot sauce or chili flakes for an extra kick of flavor.

Storage: Best eaten fresh but can be stored in the fridge for up to 2 days.

Nutritional Value
- Calories: 380
- Protein: 25g
- Fat: 31g
- Carbs: 5g

Creamy Spinach and Cheese Egg Bake

This rich and creamy egg bake combines nutritious spinach and gooey cheese, making it a satisfying and flavorful breakfast option that's low in carbs but full of flavor.

Ingredients
- 6 large eggs
- 1 cup fresh spinach, chopped
- ½ cup heavy cream
- ½ cup shredded mozzarella cheese
- 1 tbsp butter
- Salt and pepper to taste

Procedure
1. Preheat the oven to 350°F (175°C).

2. Sauté spinach in butter until wilted, then set aside.

3. Whisk eggs, cream, salt, and pepper in a bowl, then stir in the spinach and mozzarella cheese.

4. Pour the mixture into a greased baking dish and bake for 20-25 minutes until set and slightly golden.

Brilliant Tip: Add a sprinkle of nutmeg or garlic powder to elevate the flavor profile.

Storage: Can be stored in the fridge for up to 3 days. Reheat individual portions as needed.

Nutritional Value
- Calories: 420
- Protein: 28g
- Fat: 35g
- Carbs: 3g

Zucchini and Egg Breakfast Skillet

A wholesome and simple breakfast skillet that combines the fiber-rich goodness of zucchini with eggs for a filling and nutritious morning meal.

Ingredients
- 3 large eggs
- 1 small zucchini, thinly sliced
- 1 tbsp olive oil
- ½ cup shredded cheddar cheese
- Salt, pepper, and paprika to taste

Procedure
1. Heat olive oil in a skillet and sauté zucchini slices until soft.
2. Crack eggs into the skillet and cook until set.
3. Top with shredded cheese, season with salt, pepper, and paprika, and serve hot.

Brilliant Tip: Try adding a handful of fresh herbs like parsley or basil to give it a burst of freshness.

Storage: Best eaten fresh, but leftovers can be stored for up to 1 day in the fridge.

Nutritional Value
- Calories: 360
- Protein: 23g
- Fat: 30g

- Carbs: 6g

Spicy Keto Deviled Eggs

These keto-friendly deviled eggs are infused with a spicy kick, making them a quick, satisfying breakfast that's low in carbs but big on flavor.

Ingredients
- 6 large hard-boiled eggs
- 2 tbsp mayonnaise
- 1 tsp Dijon mustard
- 1 tsp hot sauce
- Paprika for garnish
- Salt and pepper to taste

Procedure
1. Peel and halve the boiled eggs, removing the yolks into a bowl.
2. Mix the yolks with mayonnaise, mustard, hot sauce, salt, and pepper until smooth.
3. Spoon the mixture back into the egg whites and garnish with paprika.

Brilliant Tip: For extra flavor, try adding a dash of smoked paprika or cayenne pepper to the filling.

Storage: Store in an airtight container in the fridge for up to 2 days.

Nutritional Value
- Calories: 250
- Protein: 12g
- Fat: 22g
- Carbs: 1g

Brilliant Tips for Success
1. Prepare in Bulk: Save time by batch cooking some of these recipes, like the egg bake or deviled eggs, so you can grab them quickly on busy mornings.

2. Prioritize Protein: Each recipe is designed to provide a balance of protein and healthy fats, helping to stabilize your blood sugar and provide sustained energy.

3. Spice Things Up: Adding different spices or herbs can completely change the flavor profile of your meals without adding carbs. Don't hesitate to experiment!

4. Stay Hydrated: Drinking water with your meals can help with digestion and keep you feeling fuller longer. Try adding a slice of lemon or cucumber for a refreshing twist.

By incorporating these energizing breakfast recipes into your Keto Egg Fast, you'll ensure you're fueling your body with the right nutrients to stay on track. These meals are quick, easy, and loaded with flavor, proving that keto-friendly breakfasts can be both delicious and satisfying!

Chapter 3

Quick and Simple Lunch Recipe

In today's busy world, it's easy to overlook lunch or grab something on the go. However, when you're following a keto egg fast, it's important to ensure your meals are not only quick but also satisfying and packed with nutrition.

Lunch plays a crucial role when you're following the Keto Egg Fast. It should be hearty enough to sustain you until dinner but light enough to keep you energized throughout the day. This chapter provides a selection of quick and simple lunch recipes that are not only delicious but also perfectly suited to your keto lifestyle. Each dish is crafted to be nutrient-rich, helping you stay in ketosis while enjoying meals that are both satisfying and flavorful.

Keto Egg Salad with a Twist

This Keto Egg Salad with a Twist offers a creamy, tangy, and rich flavor that's perfect for any keto meal. Made with high-quality fats and minimal carbs, this dish provides a hearty and fulfilling lunch to keep you satisfied and energized.

Ingredients:
- 4 large eggs, hard-boiled and chopped
- 2 tablespoons mayonnaise
- 1 tablespoon Dijon mustard
- 1 tablespoon chopped fresh dill
- 1 celery stalk, finely chopped
- Salt and pepper to taste

Instructions:
1. Mix the chopped eggs, mayonnaise, mustard, dill, and celery in a large bowl.
2. Stir until the ingredients are well combined.
3. Add salt and pepper to taste.
4. Serve over a bed of lettuce or in lettuce wraps for a low-carb option.

Storage:

Keep the egg salad in an airtight container in the refrigerator for up to 3 days. Stir before serving.

Nutritional Information (Per Serving):
- Calories: 220
- Fat: 18g
- Protein: 12g
- Carbohydrates: 2g

Spicy Deviled Eggs

These Spicy Deviled Eggs are a flavorful variation of the classic recipe. Quick to prepare and packed with healthy fats, they're ideal for a light lunch or afternoon snack. The added spice enhances metabolism, helping you stay on track with your keto goals.

Ingredients:
- 6 large eggs, hard-boiled and halved
- 3 tablespoons mayonnaise
- 1 teaspoon Dijon mustard
- 1 teaspoon hot sauce (adjust to taste)
- Paprika, for garnish

- Salt and pepper to taste

Instructions:
1. Remove the yolks from the halved eggs and place them in a bowl.
2. Mash the yolks with mayonnaise, mustard, and hot sauce until smooth.
3. Spoon the yolk mixture back into the egg whites.
4. Garnish with paprika, and season with salt and pepper.
5. Serve immediately or refrigerate before serving.

Storage:
Store in an airtight container in the fridge for up to 2 days. Best served fresh.

Nutritional Information (Per Serving):
- Calories: 140
- Fat: 12g
- Protein: 6g
- Carbohydrates: 1g

Avocado and Egg Lettuce Wraps

Avocado and Egg Lettuce Wraps combine creamy and crunchy textures, making them a delightful and satisfying keto-friendly lunch. The healthy fats from the avocado and protein from the eggs keep you full without compromising your keto diet.

Ingredients:
- 4 large eggs, hard-boiled and sliced
- 1 ripe avocado, sliced
- 6 large lettuce leaves (such as romaine or butterhead)
- 1 tablespoon mayonnaise
- Salt and pepper to taste

Instructions:
1. Spread a small amount of mayonnaise on each lettuce leaf.
2. Place slices of egg and avocado on each leaf.
3. Add salt and pepper to taste.
4. Roll the lettuce leaves to create wraps and secure them with toothpicks if needed.

Storage:

Best enjoyed fresh. However, you can prepare the ingredients ahead of time and assemble just before eating.

Nutritional Information (Per Serving):
- Calories: 250
- Fat: 21g
- Protein: 10g
- Carbohydrates: 4g

Cheesy Egg Frittata

The Cheesy Egg Frittata is a versatile, easy-to-make dish ideal for lunch. It's packed with protein and healthy fats, providing sustained energy throughout the day. This frittata is perfect for batch cooking and reheating during the week.

Ingredients:
- 6 large eggs
- 1/2 cup shredded cheddar cheese
- 1/4 cup heavy cream
- 1/2 cup spinach, chopped
- 1/4 cup diced bell pepper

- 2 tablespoons butter
- Salt and pepper to taste

Instructions:
1. Preheat the oven to 350°F (175°C).
2. In a large bowl, whisk together eggs, heavy cream, salt, and pepper.
3. Melt the butter in an oven-safe skillet over medium heat.
4. Add spinach and bell pepper, cooking until softened.
5. Pour the egg mixture into the skillet and sprinkle with cheese.
6. Cook for 2-3 minutes until the edges begin to set, then transfer the skillet to the oven.
7. Bake for 15-20 minutes until fully set and golden brown.
8. Cool slightly before slicing and serving.

Storage:
Store leftovers in the fridge for up to 3 days. Reheat in the oven or microwave.

Nutritional Information (Per Serving):

- Calories: 290
- Fat: 23g
- Protein: 16g
- Carbohydrates: 3g

Spinach Egg Drop Soup

Spinach Egg Drop Soup adds a keto twist to a comforting classic. It's a light, nourishing lunch option perfect for when you need something warm and satisfying without the extra carbs. The added spinach boosts its nutrient content.

Ingredients:

- 4 cups chicken broth
- 3 large eggs, beaten
- 1 cup fresh spinach, chopped
- 1 tablespoon soy sauce (or tamari for gluten-free)
- 1/2 teaspoon sesame oil
- Salt and pepper to taste

Instructions:

1. Bring the chicken broth to a simmer in a large pot.
2. Stir in soy sauce and sesame oil.
3. Slowly pour in the beaten eggs while stirring to create egg ribbons.
4. Add chopped spinach and cook until wilted.
5. Season with salt and pepper to taste, and serve hot.

Storage:

Store in the refrigerator for up to 2 days. Reheat gently on the stovetop before serving.

Nutritional Information (Per Serving):

- Calories: 130
- Fat: 7g
- Protein: 11g
- Carbohydrates: 2g

Spinach and Egg Stuffed Peppers

Spinach and Egg Stuffed Peppers are a nutritious, colorful, and satisfying lunch option. Packed with protein and fiber, they make a perfect dish to keep you full and energized. This recipe is great for meal prep and reheats well.

Ingredients:

- 4 large bell peppers, halved and seeds removed
- 6 large eggs
- 1 cup spinach, chopped
- 1/2 cup shredded mozzarella cheese
- 1/4 cup heavy cream
- Salt and pepper to taste

Instructions:

1. Preheat the oven to 375°F (190°C).
2. Place the bell pepper halves in a baking dish, cut side up.
3. Whisk together the eggs, heavy cream, spinach, cheese, salt, and pepper in a bowl.
4. Pour the mixture into the bell pepper halves.
5. Bake for 25-30 minutes until the eggs are fully set and peppers are tender.
6. Cool slightly before serving.

Storage:

Store leftovers in an airtight container in the fridge for up to 3 days. Reheat in the oven or microwave.

Nutritional Information (Per Serving):
- Calories: 200
- Fat: 14g
- Protein: 10g
- Carbohydrates: 6g

Egg and Bacon Salad with Spinach

This hearty salad blends the rich flavors of eggs and bacon with the freshness of spinach. It's a protein-packed, low-carb meal that's perfect for keeping you fueled through the day.

Ingredients
- 3 hard-boiled eggs
- 2 cooked bacon strips, crumbled
- 2 cups fresh spinach
- 1 tablespoon olive oil
- 1 tablespoon apple cider vinegar
- Salt and pepper to taste

Instructions

1. Slice the hard-boiled eggs and layer them over the spinach.
2. Top with crumbled bacon.
3. Mix olive oil and apple cider vinegar in a small bowl with salt and pepper.
4. Drizzle the dressing over the salad and toss gently.

Pro Tip: Add roasted pumpkin seeds for extra crunch and healthy fats to enhance both texture and flavor.

Nutritional Value (Per Serving):

- Calories: 350
- Fat: 28g
- Protein: 18g
- Carbohydrates: 2g

Keto Egg Wrap with Turkey and Cream Cheese

This light and fluffy egg wrap filled with turkey and cream cheese is a great keto-friendly option. It's quick to make and perfect for lunch.

Ingredients

- 2 large eggs
- 2 slices of turkey
- 1 tablespoon cream cheese
- 1 tablespoon butter for frying
- Salt and pepper to taste

Instructions

1. Whisk the eggs with salt and pepper.
2. Heat butter in a pan and pour in the egg mixture, cooking until it forms a thin wrap.
3. Flip the wrap and cook the other side.
4. Spread cream cheese on the egg wrap, layer with turkey, and roll it up.

Pro Tip: For added texture and nutrition, include avocado or spinach in the wrap.

Nutritional Value (Per Serving)

- Calories: 250
- Fat: 20g
- Protein: 15g
- Carbohydrates: 1g

Egg and Feta Stuffed Avocado

This filling and nutritious dish combines the creaminess of avocado with eggs and the tang of feta cheese for a satisfying, keto-friendly lunch.

Ingredients
- 1 ripe avocado, halved
- 2 large eggs
- 2 tablespoons feta cheese
- Salt and pepper to taste
- Fresh parsley (optional)

Instructions
1. Preheat the oven to 375°F (190°C).
2. Scoop out a small portion of the avocado to fit the eggs.
3. Place the avocado halves in a baking dish, crack an egg into each, and top with feta cheese.
4. Season with salt and pepper and bake for 15-18 minutes.
5. Garnish with parsley before serving.

Pro Tip: Sprinkle smoked paprika or chili flakes for an extra boost of flavor.

Nutritional Value (Per Serving)
- Calories: 320
- Fat: 26g
- Protein: 13g
- Carbohydrates: 4g

Keto Egg Roll in a Bowl

This simplified version of an egg roll delivers the same satisfying flavors without the carbs. It's quick, flavorful, and filling, perfect for a keto-friendly lunch.

Ingredients
- 3 scrambled eggs
- 1 cup shredded cabbage
- 1/2 cup ground pork or turke
- 1 tablespoon soy sauce or coconut aminos
- 1 tablespoon sesame oil
- 1 clove garlic, minced
- 1 tablespoon grated ginger
- Green onions and sesame seeds for garnish

Instructions

1. Cook the ground pork or turkey in a skillet until browned, then set aside.
2. Add sesame oil, garlic, and ginger to the skillet, sauté for 1 minute.
3. Stir in shredded cabbage and cook until wilted.
4. Add the scrambled eggs and pork back to the skillet along with soy sauce. Mix well.
5. Garnish with green onions and sesame seeds.

Pro Tip: For a spicy twist, add a dash of hot sauce or chili flakes.

Nutritional Value (Per Serving):

- Calories: 400
- Fat: 28g
- Protein: 20g
- Carbohydrates: 5g

In Chapter 3, these quick and simple lunch recipes are designed to make your Keto Egg Fast both enjoyable and manageable. They are ideal for busy women who want to stick to their keto goals without sacrificing taste or nutrition. Each dish is crafted to help you stay in ketosis while providing the energy and satisfaction you need to get through your day. Whether at home or on the go, these lunches will keep you on track with your keto journey. Enjoy the ease, flavor, and effectiveness of these meals as you continue on your path to health and wellness

Chapter 4

Delicious Dinners

Dinner is a moment to relax and enjoy a meal that not only delights your taste buds but also aligns with your keto goals. This chapter features a variety of scrumptious dinner recipes that emphasize the versatility of eggs within a keto diet. Each dish is designed to be both satisfying and flavorful, ensuring you remain committed to your keto lifestyle while savoring a diverse array of tastes and textures.

Cheesy Baked Eggs in Tomato Sauce

Cheesy Baked Eggs in Tomato Sauce offers a comforting blend of rich tomato flavors with creamy cheese and perfectly baked eggs. This dish is both nourishing and delectable, making it an excellent choice for a keto-friendly dinner.

Ingredients:
- 4 large eggs
- 1 cup tomato sauce (no added sugar)
- 1/2 cup shredded mozzarella cheese
- 1/4 cup grated Parmesan cheese
- 1 tablespoon olive oil
- 1/2 teaspoon dried oregano
- 1/2 teaspoon dried basil
- Salt and pepper to taste
- Fresh basil for garnish

Instructions:
1. Preheat your oven to 375°F (190°C).
2. Heat olive oil in a skillet over medium heat. Add tomato sauce and season with oregano, basil, salt, and pepper.
3. Simmer for 5 minutes, then transfer the sauce to a baking dish.
4. Create four wells in the sauce and crack an egg into each.
5. Top with mozzarella and Parmesan cheese.
6. Bake for 12-15 minutes until the egg whites are set but the yolks remain slightly runny.

7. Garnish with fresh basil before serving.

Storage:
Store in an airtight container in the refrigerator for up to 3 days. Reheat gently.

Nutritional Information (Per Serving):
- Calories: 320
- Fat: 24g
- Protein: 20g
- Carbohydrates: 8g

Tip: Add a pinch of red pepper flakes to the tomato sauce before baking for extra heat.

Garlic Butter Eggs over Zucchini Noodles

Garlic Butter Eggs over Zucchini Noodles provides a delicious low-carb alternative to traditional pasta dishes. The garlic butter sauce enriches the eggs, while zucchini noodles add a satisfying crunch, making it a refreshing and nutritious dinner option.

Ingredients:

- 4 large eggs
- 2 medium zucchinis, spiralized into noodles
- 2 tablespoons butter
- 2 cloves garlic, minced
- 1/4 cup grated Parmesan cheese
- Salt and pepper to taste
- Fresh parsley for garnish

Instructions:

1. Melt butter in a large skillet over medium heat. Add minced garlic and cook until fragrant, about 1-2 minutes.

2. Add zucchini noodles and sauté for 4-5 minutes until tender but still crisp. Remove from the skillet and set aside.

3. In the same skillet, cook eggs sunny-side up or to your preferred doneness.

4. Return the zucchini noodles to the skillet, tossing with the garlic butter.

5. Plate the zucchini noodles and top with eggs. Sprinkle with Parmesan cheese and garnish with parsley.

Storage:

Store in an airtight container in the refrigerator for up to 2 days. Reheat gently.

Nutritional Information (Per Serving):
- Calories: 290
- Fat: 22g
- Protein: 14g
- Carbohydrates: 6g

Tip: Add a few drops of sriracha or your favorite hot sauce for an extra kick.

Keto Egg Fried Rice

Keto Egg Fried Rice provides a flavorful, low-carb take on traditional fried rice. Using cauliflower rice ensures you stay within keto limits while enjoying the comforting flavors of this classic dish.

Ingredients:
- 4 large eggs, beaten
- 2 cups cauliflower rice
- 1 cup mixed vegetables (e.g., bell peppers, carrots, peas)

- 2 tablespoons coconut oil
- 2 tablespoons soy sauce (or tamari for gluten-free)
- 1 teaspoon sesame oil
- 2 green onions, chopped
- Salt and pepper to taste

Instructions:

1. Heat coconut oil in a large skillet or wok over medium heat. Add mixed vegetables and cook until tender, about 3-4 minutes.

2. Add cauliflower rice and cook for another 5 minutes, stirring frequently.

3. Push the rice and vegetables to one side and pour beaten eggs into the empty side.

4. Scramble the eggs until cooked, then mix with the rice and vegetables.

5. Stir in soy sauce, sesame oil, green onions, salt, and pepper. Cook for an additional 2 minutes.

Storage:

Store in an airtight container in the refrigerator for up to 3 days. Reheat in the microwave or on the stovetop.

Nutritional Information (Per Serving):

- Calories: 280
- Fat: 20g
- Protein: 15g
- Carbohydrates: 7g

Tip: Add a few drops of sriracha or your favorite hot sauce for an extra kick.

Egg and Spinach-Stuffed Chicken Breast

Egg and Spinach-Stuffed Chicken Breast pairs tender chicken with a flavorful egg and spinach filling. This dish is perfect for a special dinner or as a meal prep option, offering both taste and nutritional benefits.

Ingredients:

- 4 large chicken breasts
- 4 large eggs, hard-boiled and chopped
- 1 cup fresh spinach, chopped
- 1/2 cup shredded mozzarella cheese
- 2 tablespoons olive oil

- 1 teaspoon garlic powder
- 1 teaspoon onion powder
- Salt and pepper to taste

Instructions:

1. Preheat the oven to 375°F (190°C).
2. In a bowl, combine chopped eggs, spinach, and mozzarella cheese. Season with salt and pepper.
3. Cut a pocket into each chicken breast carefully.
4. Stuff each pocket with the egg and spinach mixture.
5. Rub the chicken with olive oil, garlic powder, onion powder, salt, and pepper.
6. Place in a baking dish and bake for 25-30 minutes, or until the chicken is fully cooked.

Storage:

Store in an airtight container in the refrigerator for up to 3 days. Reheat in the oven for best results.

Nutritional Information (Per Serving):

- Calories: 320
- Fat: 22g
- Protein: 30g

- Carbohydrates: 4g

<u>**Tip**</u>: Serve with a side of roasted vegetables for a complete meal.

Eggplant Parmesan with a Keto Egg Twist

Eggplant Parmesan with a Keto Egg Twist reimagines the classic Italian dish with a low-carb approach. The use of eggs to create a crispy coating for the eggplant provides a delicious and satisfying alternative to traditional breading.

<u>Ingredients</u>:
- 1 large eggplant, sliced into rounds
- 2 large eggs, beaten
- 1 cup almond flour
- 1 cup marinara sauce (no added sugar)
- 1 cup shredded mozzarella cheese
- 1/4 cup grated Parmesan cheese
- 2 tablespoons olive oil
- Salt and pepper to taste
- Fresh basil for garnish

Instructions:
1. Preheat your oven to 375°F (190°C).
2. Dip eggplant slices in beaten eggs, then coat with almond flour.
3. Heat olive oil in a skillet over medium heat and cook eggplant slices until golden brown.
4. Arrange the eggplant in a baking dish. Top with marinara sauce, mozzarella, and Parmesan cheese.
5. Bake for 20-25 minutes until the cheese is melted and bubbly.
6. Garnish with fresh basil before serving.

Storage:
Store leftovers in an airtight container in the refrigerator for up to 3 days. Reheat in the oven.

Nutritional Information (Per Serving):
- Calories: 290
- Fat: 22g
- Protein: 15g
- Carbohydrates: 9g

Tip: Sprinkle Italian seasoning over the eggplant before baking for added flavor.

Creamy Egg and Mushroom Casserole

Creamy Egg and Mushroom Casserole is a hearty and comforting dish that combines eggs and mushrooms in a rich, creamy sauce. It's perfect for a satisfying dinner and can be made ahead for a convenient meal option.

Ingredients:

- 6 large eggs
- 1 cup mushrooms, sliced
- 1/2 cup heavy cream
- 1/2 cup shredded cheddar cheese
- 1 tablespoon butter
- 1/2 teaspoon dried thyme
- Salt and pepper to taste

Instructions:

1. Preheat your oven to 350°F (175°C).

2. Melt butter in a skillet over medium heat. Add mushrooms and cook until tender.

3. In a bowl, whisk together eggs, heavy cream, thyme, salt, and pepper.

4. Stir in the cooked mushrooms and shredded cheddar cheese.

5. Pour into a greased baking dish and bake for 25-30 minutes until set and golden.

Storage:

Store in an airtight container in the refrigerator for up to 3 days. Reheat gently.

Nutritional Information (Per Serving):

- Calories: 310
- Fat: 25g
- Protein: 17g
- Carbohydrates: 4g

Tip: Add a handful of fresh spinach or chopped herbs for extra nutrition and flavor.

Baked Eggs with Spinach and Parmesan

This simple yet nutritious dish brings together the rich flavors of baked eggs, spinach, and Parmesan cheese. It's a high-protein, low-carb dinner that fits perfectly into your keto egg fast plan.

Ingredients
- 4 large eggs
- 2 cups fresh spinach
- 1/4 cup grated Parmesan cheese
- 1 tablespoon butter
- Salt and pepper to taste

Directions
1. Preheat your oven to 375°F (190°C).
2. Grease a baking dish with butter and spread the spinach evenly at the bottom.
3. Crack the eggs over the spinach and sprinkle with Parmesan, salt, and pepper.
4. Bake for 15-20 minutes, or until the eggs reach your desired doneness.
5. Serve immediately, with extra Parmesan if desired.

Tip: For added flavor, pair this dish with sautéed mushrooms or slices of avocado.

Nutritional Info (Per Serving)
- Calories: 250

- Protein: 18g
- Fat: 20g
- Carbs: 3g

Keto Eggplant and Egg Casserole

This hearty casserole combines tender eggplant with rich eggs and cheese. It's a comforting, low-carb dinner that will leave you feeling satisfied while keeping you in ketosis.

Ingredients
- 2 medium eggplants, sliced
- 6 large eggs
- 1/2 cup shredded mozzarella cheese
- 1/4 cup grated Parmesan cheese
- 2 tablespoons olive oil
- Salt, pepper, and Italian seasoning to taste

Directions
1. Preheat the oven to 400°F (200°C).
2. Arrange eggplant slices on a baking sheet, brush with olive oil, and sprinkle with salt. Roast for 20 minutes, flipping halfway.

3. In a greased casserole dish, layer the roasted eggplant, eggs, and cheese, seasoning each layer with salt, pepper, and Italian seasoning.
4. Bake for 25-30 minutes, or until the cheese is golden and bubbling.
5. Let cool slightly before serving.

Tip: Sprinkle some red pepper flakes for a bit of heat. This is a great recipe for batch cooking, so you can enjoy it throughout the week.

Nutritional Info (Per Serving)
- Calories: 280
- Protein: 16g
- Fat: 22g
- Carbs: 7g

Spicy Shrimp and Egg Stir-Fry
For seafood lovers, this spicy shrimp and egg stir-fry is the perfect dish to enjoy on your keto egg fast. Packed with protein and low in carbs, it's a flavorful way to stick to your keto goals.

Ingredients

- 8 large shrimp, peeled and deveined
- 4 large eggs
- 1 tablespoon coconut oil
- 1/2 red bell pepper, sliced
- 1/2 onion, sliced
- 1 clove garlic, minced
- 1 teaspoon red pepper flake
- Salt and pepper to taste

Directions:

1. Heat coconut oil in a skillet over medium heat. Add the garlic, onion, and bell pepper, and cook until softened.

2. Push the veggies to one side of the skillet and scramble the eggs on the other side until fully cooked.

3. Add the shrimp to the skillet, sprinkle with red pepper flakes, salt, and pepper, and cook until the shrimp are pink and firm.

4. Stir everything together and serve hot.

Tip: For a milder flavor, reduce the amount of red pepper flakes or leave them out. You can also toss in a handful of spinach or kale for extra nutrients.

Nutritional Info (Per Serving)
- Calories: 300
- Protein: 27g
- Fat: 20g
- Carbs: 4g

Keto Egg Lasagna

Enjoy the flavors of lasagna while staying in ketosis with this egg-based version. By swapping out traditional noodles for layers of eggs and cheese, this keto-friendly lasagna is the perfect low-carb dinner.

Ingredients
- 6 large eggs
- 1 cup ricotta cheese
- 1/2 cup shredded mozzarella cheese
- 1/2 cup grated Parmesan cheese
- 1 cup marinara sauce (no sugar added)
- 1 tablespoon olive oil
- Salt, pepper, and Italian seasoning to taste

Directions

1. Preheat the oven to 350°F (175°C).

2. Whisk the eggs in a bowl, season with salt and pepper, and pour into a greased baking dish. Bake for about 10 minutes, or until set.

3. In a casserole dish, layer the baked egg, ricotta cheese, marinara sauce, and mozzarella, seasoning each layer with Italian seasoning.

4. Repeat until all ingredients are used, topping with Parmesan.

5. Bake for 25-30 minutes, or until the cheese is golden and bubbly.

Tip: This lasagna freezes well, making it ideal for meal prep. You can also add ground beef or sausage for additional protein.

Nutritional Info (Per Serving)

- Calories: 350
- Protein: 22g
- Fat: 28g
- Carbs: 6g

As we wrap up this chapter, remember that dinner can be both simple and extraordinary. These egg-based recipes are designed to make your keto journey deliciously satisfying while offering a variety of flavors and textures. Whether you're enjoying a comforting Cheesy Baked Egg dish or savoring the savory Garlic Butter Eggs over Zucchini Noodles, these meals ensure that you remain committed to your keto goals without sacrificing taste. Embrace the versatility of eggs and let these dishes transform your dinners into delightful, healthful experiences.

Chapter 5

Satisfying Snacks and Small Plates

Maintaining your ketogenic goals doesn't mean you have to sacrifice flavor or satisfaction. In this chapter, we focus on egg-based snacks and small plates that are perfect for keeping hunger at bay and aligning with your Keto Egg Fast. These recipes are crafted to be delicious and fulfilling, ensuring you stay on track with your dietary goals while enjoying every bite.

Parmesan-Crusted Deviled Eggs

Elevate the classic deviled eggs with a Parmesan crust for a savory snack that's rich and satisfying. These Parmesan-Crusted Deviled Eggs provide a delightful twist on a familiar favorite, combining creamy filling with a crisp, cheesy topping.

Ingredients:

- 6 large eggs
- 2 tablespoons mayonnaise
- 1 teaspoon Dijon mustard
- 1 tablespoon chopped fresh chives
- 1/4 cup grated Parmesan cheese
- Salt and pepper, to taste

Procedure:

1. Hard boil the eggs: Place them in a pot, cover with water, and bring to a boil. Once boiling, cover the pot and let the eggs sit for 12 minutes. Transfer to an ice bath to cool.

2. Peel the eggs and cut them in half. Remove the yolks and mash them in a bowl. Mix with mayonnaise, Dijon mustard, chives, salt, and pepper.

3. Spoon or pipe the yolk mixture back into the egg whites.

4. Sprinkle Parmesan cheese on top and broil for 2-3 minutes, until golden.

Method of Storage:
Keep leftovers in an airtight container in the refrigerator for up to 3 days.

Nutritional Value:
- About 90 calories
- 7g fat
- 1g carbs
- 6g protein per serving.

Tip: Enhance the flavor with a touch of paprika or crumbled bacon before broiling.

Egg and Cheese Keto Bites

Egg and Cheese Keto Bites are convenient, protein-packed snacks perfect for a busy day. These mini treats blend eggs and cheese into satisfying bites that are both nutritious and easy to prepare.

Ingredients:
- 6 large eggs
- 1 cup shredded cheddar cheese
- 1/2 cup diced bell peppers
- 1/4 cup chopped green onions

- Salt and pepper, to taste

Procedure:
1. Preheat the oven to 350°F (175°C) and grease a mini muffin tin.
2. Whisk the eggs and stir in the cheddar cheese, bell peppers, and green onions. Season with salt and pepper.
3. Pour the mixture into the muffin tin, filling each cup about 3/4 full.
4. Bake for 15-20 minutes, until set and lightly golden.

Method of Storage:
Store in an airtight container in the refrigerator for up to 5 days or freeze for up to 1 month.

Nutritional Value:
- Approximately 70 calories
- 5g fat
- 1g carbs
- 5g protein per serving.

Tip: Add your favorite keto-friendly vegetables or herbs to personalize these bites.

Keto Egg Chips with Dipping Sauce

Keto Egg Chips provide a crunchy, low-carb alternative to traditional chips, making them a great choice for snacking or pairing with a savory dip. They're perfect for satisfying your cravings while staying keto-compliant.

Ingredients:
- 4 large eggs
- 1/2 cup grated Parmesan cheese
- 1 teaspoon dried oregano
- Salt and pepper, to taste

Procedure:
1. Preheat the oven to 375°F (190°C) and line a baking sheet with parchment paper.
2. Whisk the eggs until frothy and mix in the Parmesan cheese, oregano, salt, and pepper.
3. Spread the egg mixture thinly onto the parchment paper in a uniform layer.

4. Bake for 10-12 minutes, until crispy and golden. Cool slightly before cutting into chip-sized pieces.

Method of Storage:
Store in an airtight container at room temperature for up to 2 days, or in the refrigerator for longer storage.

Nutritional Value:
- About 80 calories
- 6g fat
- 1g carbs
- 6g protein per serving.

Tip: Serve with a keto-friendly dipping sauce like garlic aioli or creamy avocado dip for added flavor.

Spinach and Egg Fat Bombs

Spinach and Egg Fat Bombs are nutrient-dense snacks rich in healthy fats and greens. They are perfect for a quick energy boost and are aligned with your keto dietary needs.

Ingredients:
- 4 large eggs
- 1 cup fresh spinach, chopped
- 1/4 cup cream cheese
- 1/4 cup grated cheddar cheese
- Salt and pepper, to taste

Procedure:
1. Preheat the oven to 350°F (175°C) and grease a mini muffin tin.
2. Sauté the spinach until wilted and set aside.
3. In a bowl, whisk the eggs and mix in cream cheese, cheddar cheese, spinach, salt, and pepper.
4. Pour the mixture into the mini muffin tin and bake for 15-20 minutes, until set and golden.

Method of Storage:
Keep in an airtight container in the refrigerator for up to 5 days.

Nutritional Value:
- Approximately 90 calories
- 7g fat
- 2g carbs

- 6g protein per serving.

Tip: Customize with different cheeses or herbs to suit your taste preferences.

Spicy Egg Avocado Dip

Spicy Egg Avocado Dip combines the creaminess of avocado with the protein of eggs, creating a zesty and satisfying dip. It's perfect for pairing with veggies or keto crackers.

Ingredients:
- 2 ripe avocados
- 2 hard-boiled eggs, chopped
- 1 tablespoon lime juice
- 1/4 cup chopped cilantro
- 1 small jalapeño, seeded and minced
- Salt and pepper, to taste

Procedure:
1. Mash the avocados with lime juice until smooth.
2. Fold in the chopped eggs, cilantro, jalapeño, salt, and pepper.
3. Serve immediately with keto-friendly dippers.

Method of Storage:

Store in an airtight container in the refrigerator for up to 2 days. The dip may brown slightly but is still safe to eat.

Nutritional Value:

- About 150 calories
- 12g fat
- 8g carbs
- 6g protein per serving.

Tip: Add smoked paprika or hot sauce for extra flavor.

Egg White and Cheese Crisps

Egg White and Cheese Crisps are a crunchy, low-carb snack that offers a satisfying crunch while staying keto-friendly. They're perfect for a quick snack that won't derail your dietary goals.

Ingredients:

- 4 egg whites
- 1/2 cup shredded mozzarella cheese

- 1/4 teaspoon garlic powder
- 1/4 teaspoon onion powder
- Salt and pepper, to taste

Procedure:

1. Preheat the oven to 375°F (190°C) and line a baking sheet with parchment paper.
2. Whisk the egg whites until frothy and mix in shredded mozzarella, garlic powder, onion powder, salt, and pepper.
3. Drop spoonfuls of the mixture onto the parchment paper, spreading into thin circles.
4. Bake for 10-12 minutes, until the crisps are golden and crunchy.

Method of Storage:

Store in an airtight container at room temperature for up to 3 days.

Nutritional Value:

- About 70 calories
- 4g fat
- 1g carbs
- 7g protein per serving.

Tip: Enhance with herbs or red pepper flakes before baking for added flavor.

Buffalo Egg-Stuffed Celery Sticks

This snack pairs the bold flavor of buffalo sauce with the crunch of celery. These celery sticks stuffed with egg are both flavorful and a great way to get in some extra protein between meals.

Ingredients
- 4 hard-boiled eggs
- 1/4 cup buffalo sauce
- 4 celery sticks
- 2 tbsp cream cheese
- Salt and pepper to taste

Instructions
1. Mash the hard-boiled eggs with cream cheese and buffalo sauce until smooth.
2. Add salt and pepper to taste.
3. Fill the celery sticks with the egg mixture and serve.

Pro Tip:

For added texture, sprinkle some chopped bacon or fresh chives on top for extra flavor without adding unnecessary carbs.

Nutritional Information (per serving):
- Calories: 150
- Fat: 12g
- Protein: 10g
- Carbs: 2g

Keto Egg Cloud Bites

These light and fluffy egg cloud bites make a perfect snack to curb your cravings while keeping you in ketosis. They're quick to make and filled with protein.

Ingredients
- 4 large eggs
- 1/4 cup shredded cheddar cheese
- 1/4 tsp garlic powder
- 1/4 tsp paprika
- Salt and pepper to taste

Instructions

1. Preheat the oven to 350°F (175°C). Separate the egg whites from the yolks.
2. Whisk the egg whites until they form stiff peaks. Gently fold in the cheese, garlic powder, paprika, salt, and pepper.
3. Drop spoonfuls of the mixture onto a baking sheet and bake for 10-12 minutes until golden.

Pro Tip:

Make extra and store them in the fridge for up to three days. They reheat well and are a convenient on-the-go snack.

Nutritional Information (per serving):

- Calories: 120
- Fat: 8g
- Protein: 9g
- Carbs: 1g

Roasted Egg-Stuffed Mushrooms

These savory mushrooms are stuffed with a delicious egg and cheese mixture, creating a warm, bite-sized snack that's both filling and flavorful.

Ingredients

- 8 large button mushrooms
- 2 hard-boiled eggs, mashed
- 1/4 cup shredded mozzarella
- 1 tbsp mayonnaise
- Salt and pepper to taste
- Chopped parsley for garnish

Instructions

1. Preheat the oven to 375°F (190°C). Remove the stems from the mushrooms and scoop out a little to make space for the filling.
2. Mix the mashed eggs, cheese, mayonnaise, salt, and pepper together.
3. Fill each mushroom with the mixture and bake for 15-18 minutes until the mushrooms are tender and the cheese is golden.
4. Garnish with parsley and serve.

Pro Tip:

Add a dash of hot sauce to the filling for a spicy twist, or substitute mozzarella with feta for a tangier flavor.

Nutritional Information (per serving):

- Calories: 180
- Fat: 14g
- Protein: 11g
- Carbs: 2g

Crispy Parmesan Egg Chips

These crunchy egg chips are a satisfying snack that keeps you on track with your keto diet. Made from simple ingredients, they offer the perfect alternative to traditional chips.

Ingredients

- 4 large eggs
- 1/4 cup grated Parmesan cheese
- 1/4 tsp black pepper
- 1/4 tsp smoked paprika

Instructions

1. Preheat the oven to 400°F (200°C) and line a baking sheet with parchment paper.
2. Whisk the eggs with Parmesan cheese, pepper, and paprika.

3. Spoon small amounts onto the baking sheet, spreading them into thin circles.

4. Bake for 8-10 minutes until crispy and golden.

Pro Tip:
Pair these chips with a keto-friendly dip like guacamole or sour cream for an extra layer of flavor.

Nutritional Information (per serving):
- Calories: 100
- Fat: 7g
- Protein: 8g
- Carbs: 1g

This chapter showcases a range of egg-based snacks and small plates designed to support your ketogenic lifestyle while keeping you satisfied. Each recipe is crafted to ensure you enjoy flavorful, fulfilling options that align with your keto goals. Always listen to your body and use these snacks in moderation to fuel your keto journey effectively. By incorporating these snacks into your diet, you can maintain your commitment to the Keto Egg Fast, enjoy a variety of tastes, and stay energized throughout the day. Embrace these delicious choices as part of your journey and celebrate the convenience and pleasure they bring to your keto experience.

Chapter 7

Indulgent Desserts

In this chapter, we explore how to satisfy your sweet cravings while staying true to your keto goals. Each dessert is crafted to be both delicious and in harmony with your ketogenic lifestyle. These recipes are designed to bring you joy without derailing your progress, offering a blend of indulgence and nutrition. Enjoy these sweet treats knowing they're perfectly suited to your keto journey.

Vanilla Egg Custard

Vanilla egg custard is a classic dessert with a keto twist, delivering creamy, rich flavor that's perfect for ending any meal on a high note. This recipe combines the comforting taste of vanilla with the principles of keto for a truly satisfying treat.

Ingredients
- 4 large eggs
- 1 ½ cups unsweetened almond milk
- ¼ cup granulated erythritol
- 1 tsp vanilla extract
- ¼ tsp salt
- A pinch of nutmeg (optional)

Procedure
1. Preheat your oven to 325°F (163°C).
2. In a bowl, whisk together eggs, erythritol, and salt until blended.
3. Gradually mix in the almond milk and vanilla extract.
4. Pour the mixture into custard cups or a baking dish.
5. Place these cups in a larger baking dish and add hot water halfway up the sides.
6. Bake for 30-35 minutes, or until the custard is set and a knife inserted in the center comes out clean.
7. Cool and refrigerate for at least an hour before serving.

Method of Storage
Refrigerate in an airtight container for up to 5 days.

Nutritional Value
- Calories: 150
- Fat: 11g
- Carbohydrates: 6g
- Protein: 6g

Chocolate Egg Pudding
Rich and creamy, chocolate egg pudding offers a keto-friendly way to enjoy a chocolatey dessert. This pudding combines eggs with cocoa to create a luscious treat perfect for any chocolate lover.

Ingredients
- 4 large eggs
- 1 ¼ cups unsweetened almond milk
- ¼ cup unsweetened cocoa powder
- ¼ cup granulated erythritol
- 1 tsp vanilla extract
- A pinch of salt

Procedure

1. Heat almond milk in a saucepan over medium heat until hot but not boiling.
2. Whisk eggs, cocoa powder, erythritol, and salt in a bowl until smooth.
3. Slowly add the hot milk to the egg mixture, whisking constantly.
4. Return the mixture to the saucepan and cook over medium heat, stirring constantly, until thickened.
5. Stir in vanilla extract and remove from heat.
6. Pour into serving dishes and cool before refrigerating.

Method of Storage

Refrigerate for up to 4 days.

Nutritional Value

- Calories: 180
- Fat: 14g
- Carbohydrates: 7g
- Protein: 8g

Lemon Keto Egg Bars

Bright and tangy lemon keto egg bars are a refreshing and light dessert option. These bars are perfect for those who enjoy a citrusy treat while adhering to their keto diet.

Ingredients
- 4 large eggs
- ½ cup unsweetened almond milk
- ¼ cup lemon juice
- ¼ cup granulated erythritol
- 2 tbsp coconut flour
- 1 tsp lemon zest
- 1 tsp baking powder
- ¼ tsp salt

Procedure
1. Preheat your oven to 350°F (175°C). Line an 8x8-inch baking pan with parchment paper.
2. Whisk together eggs, almond milk, lemon juice, and erythritol in a bowl.
3. Add coconut flour, lemon zest, baking powder, and salt, mixing until smooth.
4. Pour the batter into the prepared pan.

5. Bake for 25-30 minutes, or until the bars are set and lightly golden.
6. Cool completely before cutting into squares.

Method of Storage
Keep in an airtight container at room temperature for up to 3 days or refrigerate for up to a week.

Nutritional Value
- Calories: 120
- Fat: 10g
- Carbohydrates: 5g
- Protein: 6g

Cinnamon-Spiced Egg Pancakes

Cinnamon-spiced egg pancakes offer a sweet and satisfying way to indulge while staying keto-compliant. These pancakes have a delightful texture and flavor, making them a great choice for a light dessert or snack.

Ingredients
- 4 large eggs
- 2 tbsp almond flour

- 1 tsp cinnamon
- 1 tbsp granulated erythritol
- 1 tsp vanilla extract
- Butter or oil for cooking

Procedure

1. Whisk together eggs, almond flour, cinnamon, erythritol, and vanilla extract in a bowl.
2. Heat a skillet over medium heat with a small amount of butter or oil.
3. Pour batter into the skillet to form small pancakes.
4. Cook for 2-3 minutes on each side until golden brown.
5. Serve warm with extra cinnamon or keto-friendly whipped cream if desired.

Method of Storage

Refrigerate for up to 3 days and reheat in a skillet or microwave.

Nutritional Value

- Calories: 140
- Fat: 10g

- Carbohydrates: 5g
- Protein: 8g

Egg Fast Cheesecake Bites

Egg fast cheesecake bites are small, creamy delights perfect for a quick dessert. These bites are easy to make and provide a rich, satisfying treat that fits perfectly into your keto plan.

Ingredients
- 4 oz cream cheese, softened
- 2 large eggs
- ¼ cup granulated erythritol
- 1 tsp vanilla extract

Procedure
1. Preheat your oven to 325°F (163°C). Line a mini muffin tin with paper liners.
2. Beat cream cheese until smooth.
3. Mix in eggs, erythritol, and vanilla extract until well combined.
4. Pour the mixture into the mini muffin tin, filling each cup about ¾ full.

5. Bake for 15-20 minutes, until set and lightly golden.

6. Cool and refrigerate for at least 1 hour before serving.

Method of Storage

Refrigerate for up to a week.

Nutritional Value

- Calories: 120
- Fat: 10g
- Carbohydrates: 3g
- Protein: 5g

Coconut Egg Pudding

Coconut egg pudding offers a smooth and creamy dessert with a hint of tropical flavor. This pudding blends the richness of coconut with the smooth texture of egg custard for a delicious keto-friendly treat.

Ingredients

- 4 large eggs
- 1 cup coconut milk

- ¼ cup granulated erythritol
- 1 tsp vanilla extract
- A pinch of sea salt

Procedure

1. Preheat your oven to 325°F (163°C).
2. In a bowl, mix eggs, coconut milk, erythritol, and sea salt until smooth.
3. Pour the mixture into custard cups or ramekins.
4. Place the cups in a larger baking dish and add hot water halfway up the sides.
5. Bake for 30-35 minutes, or until set and slightly golden on top.
6. Cool and refrigerate for at least 2 hours before serving.

Method of Storage

Refrigerate for up to 5 days.

Nutritional Value

- Calories: 160
- Fat: 14g
- Carbohydrates: 6g
- Protein: 5g

Keto Cinnamon Egg Soufflé

Experience the fluffy, comforting delight of this Keto Cinnamon Egg Soufflé. Its warm, spiced flavor makes it an ideal treat when you're seeking a sweet yet keto-compliant dessert.

Ingredients

- 4 large eggs
- 1/4 cup heavy cream
- 1/4 cup erythritol (or other keto-friendly sweetener)
- 1 tsp ground cinnamon
- 1/2 tsp vanilla extract
- A pinch of salt
- Butter for greasing

Instructions

1. Preheat your oven to 375°F (190°C) and grease ramekins with butter.
2. In a bowl, mix eggs, heavy cream, erythritol, cinnamon, vanilla, and salt until smooth.
3. Pour the mixture into the ramekins.

4. Set the ramekins in a baking dish and add hot water halfway up the sides (creating a water bath).
5. Bake for 20-25 minutes until puffed and golden.
6. Let cool slightly before serving.

Pro Tip: For extra flavor, consider adding a pinch of nutmeg or sprinkling chopped nuts on top before baking.

Nutritional Information (per serving)
- Calories: 250
- Fat: 22g
- Protein: 9g
- Carbs: 5g (Net Carbs: 3g)

Egg Fast Lemon Mousse
Brighten up your day with this Egg Fast Lemon Mousse, a tangy and creamy dessert that's light yet incredibly satisfying.

Ingredients
- 3 large egg yolks
- 1/4 cup freshly squeezed lemon juice
- 1/4 cup powdered erythritol

- 1/2 cup heavy cream
- 1 tsp lemon zest
- A pinch of salt

Instructions

1. Heat egg yolks, lemon juice, and erythritol in a saucepan over low heat, stirring constantly until thickened.
2. Remove from heat and cool.
3. Whip the heavy cream until stiff peaks form.
4. Gently fold the cooled lemon mixture into the whipped cream.
5. Spoon into serving dishes and chill for at least 2 hours.

Pro Tip: Garnish with additional lemon zest or a sprig of mint for added freshness and visual appeal.

Nutritional Information (per serving)

- Calories: 220
- Fat: 20g
- Protein: 4g
- Carbs: 6g (Net Carbs: 4g)

Keto Chocolate Egg Truffles

Treat yourself to these Keto Chocolate Egg Truffles, a rich and indulgent snack that satisfies your chocolate cravings while keeping you within keto limits.

Ingredients
- 1/2 cup heavy cream
- 1/2 cup unsweetened cocoa powder
- 1/4 cup erythritol (or other keto-friendly sweetener)
- 2 large egg yolks
- 1/4 cup chopped nuts (optional)
- 1/4 tsp vanilla extract

Instructions
1. Simmer heavy cream in a saucepan, then remove from heat.
2. Stir in cocoa powder and erythritol until smooth.
3. Mix in egg yolks and vanilla extract.
4. Chill until firm.
5. Form into small balls and roll in chopped nuts if desired.

Pro Tip: For a gourmet touch, coat the truffles in unsweetened cocoa powder or melted keto chocolate before serving.

Nutritional Information (per serving)
- Calories: 150
- Fat: 14g
- Protein: 4g
- Carbs: 5g (Net Carbs: 3g)

Vanilla and Coconut Egg Custard

Enjoy the creamy, comforting flavors of Vanilla and Coconut Egg Custard. This delightful dessert combines vanilla and coconut for a rich, satisfying treat that fits perfectly into your keto plan.

Ingredients
- 4 large eggs
- 1 cup full-fat coconut milk
- 1/4 cup erythritol (or other keto-friendly sweetener)
- 1 tsp vanilla extract
- 1/4 cup shredded unsweetened coconut
- A pinch of salt

Instructions

1. Preheat oven to 350°F (175°C) and grease ramekins.
2. Combine eggs, coconut milk, erythritol, vanilla, and salt in a bowl.
3. Stir in shredded coconut.
4. Pour into ramekins.
5. Place ramekins in a baking dish and add hot water halfway up the sides.
6. Bake for 25-30 minutes, or until set and lightly golden.
7. Cool before serving.

Pro Tip: Enhance the custard with toasted coconut flakes for added texture and flavor.

Nutritional Information (per serving)

- Calories: 210
- Fat: 18g
- Protein: 6g
- Carbs: 6g (Net Carbs: 4g)

Incorporating these indulgent desserts into your keto egg fast can add a touch of sweetness and celebration to your journey. Each recipe is crafted to align with your keto goals while offering satisfying, flavorful options. Enjoy these treats as a reward for your dedication and a reminder that you can delight in sweet moments without straying from your path. Let these desserts be a part of your success story, making your keto journey not just manageable, but also truly enjoyable.

Chapter 7

Keto Egg Fast Meal Plans

Welcome to Chapter 7 of *"The Keto Egg Fast Diet Cookbook for Women: Simple Healthy Egg-Centric Meals to Boost Your Keto Journey."* This chapter offers structured meal plans and guidance to ensure a seamless and effective egg fast experience. Whether you're just beginning or aiming to refine your approach, these plans will help you achieve your keto goals.

3-Day Rapid Start Meal Plan

Day 1:

Breakfast: Classic Butter Scrambled Eggs
- Savor the richness of scrambled eggs cooked in ample butter for added flavor and fat.

Lunch: Egg Salad with a Keto Twist
- Blend chopped hard-boiled eggs with mayo, mustard, and fresh herbs for a creamy, satisfying meal.

Dinner: Garlic Butter Eggs over Zucchini Noodles
- Sauté eggs in garlic butter and serve over spiralized zucchini noodles for a delicious, low-carb dinner.

Day 2:

Breakfast: Fluffy Cheese Omelette
- Enjoy a light and fluffy omelette packed with cheese to keep you full and energized.

Lunch: Avocado and Egg Lettuce Wraps
- Pair hard-boiled egg slices with creamy avocado in crisp lettuce wraps.

Dinner: Keto Egg Fried Rice
- Use cauliflower rice as a base, and mix in scrambled eggs, soy sauce, and veggies for a flavorful, egg-focused meal.

Day 3:

Breakfast: Spinach and Mushroom Egg Muffins
- Bake a mixture of eggs, spinach, and mushrooms in muffin tins for a convenient, nutrient-rich breakfast.

Lunch: Deviled Eggs with a Kick
- Add a dash of paprika and hot sauce to deviled eggs for extra flavor.

Dinner: Cheesy Baked Eggs in Tomato Sauce
- Enjoy baked eggs in a savory tomato sauce topped with melted cheese for a comforting meal.

5-Day Egg Fast Meal Plan

Day 1:

Breakfast: Egg and Cheese Chaffles
- Create savory waffles from eggs and cheese for a quick, satisfying breakfast.

Lunch: Egg Drop Soup with a Spin
- Relish a bowl of egg drop soup enhanced with added spinach for extra nutrients.

Dinner: Eggplant Parmesan with a Keto Egg Twist
- Layer baked eggplant with eggs and cheese for a keto-friendly take on this classic dish.

Day 2:

Breakfast: Keto Pancakes with Egg Base
- Enjoy pancakes made from an egg-based recipe, topped with butter for a hearty breakfast.

Lunch: Egg and Spinach Stuffed Peppers
- Fill bell peppers with a mix of eggs and spinach, then bake until tender.

Dinner: Egg and Spinach-Stuffed Chicken Breast
- Stuff chicken breasts with a flavorful egg and spinach mixture and bake to perfection.

Day 3:

Breakfast: Bacon-Wrapped Egg Cups
- Wrap eggs in bacon and bake for a flavorful breakfast option.

Lunch: Cheesy Egg Frittata

- Prepare a frittata filled with cheese and keto-friendly vegetables.

Dinner: Creamy Egg and Mushroom Casserole
- Bake eggs with mushrooms and a creamy sauce for a comforting, satisfying dinner.

Day 4:

Breakfast: Spicy Egg Avocado Dip
- Combine eggs with avocado and spices for a spicy, creamy breakfast dip.

Lunch: Egg White and Cheese Crisps
- Bake egg whites with cheese to create crispy, savory snacks.

Dinner: Garlic Butter Eggs over Zucchini Noodles (Repeat from Day 1)

Day 5:

Breakfast: Vanilla Egg Custard
- Indulge in a vanilla-flavored egg custard that remains keto-friendly.

Lunch: Egg Salad with a Keto Twist (Repeat from Day 1)

Dinner: Keto Egg Fried Rice (Repeat from Day 2)

How to Transition Back to Regular Keto

After completing your egg fast, reintroduce other keto-friendly foods gradually. Start with low-carb vegetables, healthy fats, and lean proteins. Pay attention to how your body reacts and adjust your meals to maintain your progress and nutritional balance.

Some examples of low-carb vegetables include:

- Zucchini
- Spinach
- Cauliflower
- Avocado
- Broccoli

Long-Term Keto Success Strategies

1. **Stay Consistent:** Keep a regular meal schedule and adhere to keto-friendly foods to maintain fat-burning mode.

2. **Hydrate Well**: Drink plenty of water and consider electrolyte-rich foods or supplements to prevent deficiencies.
3. **Tune Into Your Body:** Notice how different foods affect your energy and overall well-being. Adjust your diet based on personal responses.
4. **Seek Community Support:** Join keto groups or find a support network to share experiences, tips, and motivation.

Embarking on the keto egg fast is a powerful step towards transformation. The meal plans and strategies in this chapter are crafted to simplify your journey and maximize your success. Stay dedicated, listen to your body, and adapt as needed. Celebrate each achievement and keep progressing with confidence. Your path to a healthier, more vibrant you is well within reach!

Chapter 8

Troubleshooting and Tips

Starting the Keto Egg Fast can bring significant benefits, but it may come with its own set of challenges. This chapter will help you navigate common issues and provide practical advice to keep you on track and make the most of your egg-focused journey.

Common Challenges on the Egg Fast

1. Adapting to the Diet: As your body adjusts to the egg fast, you might feel tired or experience digestive changes. These are normal as your metabolism shifts. Make sure you're staying hydrated and maintaining your electrolytes. Adding a bit of salt to your meals can help balance your electrolytes.

2. Managing Hunger: You might find it hard to feel full with just eggs. To combat this, try adding high-fat ingredients like cheese or avocado to your meals. Fat helps to keep you satisfied for longer.

3. Overcoming Flavor Fatigue: Eating the same foods repeatedly can lead to boredom. Keep your meals interesting by experimenting with different herbs, spices, and cooking methods.

4. Social Situations: Attending social events while on the egg fast can be challenging. Eat a filling meal or snack before you go, and don't hesitate to explain your dietary choices to others. Most people will respect your commitment to your health.

5. Digestive Discomfort: Digestive issues may arise for some. To alleviate this, consider adding fiber from allowed low-carb vegetables or taking probiotics to support digestive health.

How to Break a Weight Loss Plateau

Weight loss plateaus are a normal part of the journey. Here's how to push through them:

1.   Reevaluate   Your   Macronutrients: Double-check that you're adhering to the correct macronutrient ratios for keto. Even small deviations can affect your progress. Use a tracking tool to monitor your intake and make adjustments if necessary.

2. Increase Physical Activity: Incorporate a mix of cardiovascular exercise and strength training to boost your metabolism and overcome plateaus. Exercise benefits both your weight loss and overall well-being.

3. Adjust Your Fast: If you've been following the egg fast for an extended period, consider reintroducing some new keto-friendly foods briefly before returning to the fast. This can help reset your metabolism and make the fast more effective.

4. Manage Stress: High stress levels can hinder weight loss. Engage in stress-reducing activities like meditation, deep breathing, or yoga to manage stress and support your weight loss goals.

5. Prioritize Quality Sleep: Inadequate sleep can impact weight loss. Aim for 7-8 hours of restful sleep each night to aid in your weight management efforts.

Managing Cravings and Staying on Track

Cravings can be a major challenge. Here's how to manage them:

1. Stay Hydrated: Sometimes cravings can be mistaken for thirst. Drink plenty of water throughout the day and consider herbal teas as a hydrating, zero-calorie option.

2. Keep Busy: Distract yourself from cravings by engaging in activities you enjoy. Staying occupied can help shift your focus away from food.

3. Practice Mindful Eating: When you do eat, focus on enjoying your food and eating slowly. Mindful eating can enhance your satisfaction with smaller portions.

4. Have Keto-Friendly Snacks Ready: Keep keto-friendly snacks like hard-boiled eggs, cheese sticks, or a small portion of nuts handy for times when cravings hit.

5. Review Your Goals: Remind yourself of the reasons you started the egg fast. Keeping your goals in mind can strengthen your commitment.

Frequently Asked Questions

1. Can I eat anything besides eggs during the fast?

The egg fast primarily focuses on eggs, but including some fats and cheese is typically acceptable. Always follow the specific guidelines of your chosen plan.

2. What if I'm not seeing the expected results?

Review your adherence to the diet, look for any deviations, and consider consulting a nutritionist for personalized guidance.

3. Is it safe to follow the egg fast for a long period?

The egg fast is generally intended for short-term use. Prolonged use might lead to nutrient deficiencies. Plan to transition back to a balanced keto diet after the fast.

4. How can I stay motivated?

Set small, attainable goals and celebrate your progress. Engaging with support groups or finding a buddy to share your journey with can provide additional motivation and accountability.

Facing challenges during the Keto Egg Fast is natural, but with the right strategies and a positive mindset, you can overcome them. Be patient with yourself, stay proactive, and use the tips provided to maintain your commitment and achieve your health goals. Embrace the journey, recognize your achievements, and stay focused on your objectives. Your dedication will lead to rewarding results and a healthier, more vibrant you.

Chapter 9

Maintaining Your Results

Congratulations on completing the Keto Egg Fast! By now, you've likely experienced the numerous benefits of this diet, from increased energy levels to noticeable weight loss. As you transition out of the egg fast, it's essential to maintain your progress and continue supporting your health goals. This chapter will provide guidance on how to reintroduce foods, establish a sustainable keto lifestyle, and keep your results over the long term.

Reintroducing Foods After the Egg Fast

After completing the egg fast, reintroducing foods should be done gradually and mindfully. Start by adding non-starchy vegetables, low-carb fruits, and lean proteins back into your diet. Focus on whole, unprocessed foods to continue providing your body with high-quality nutrients.

Tips for Reintroduction

1. **Take It Slow:** Reintroduce one new food at a time and observe how your body reacts. This will help you detect any potential food sensitivities.
2. **Listen to Your Body:** Pay close attention to how you feel after consuming new foods. This awareness will help you adjust your diet according to what suits you best.
3. **Stay Hydrated:** Keep drinking plenty of water to aid digestion and support overall health during this transition phase.

Building a Sustainable Keto Lifestyle

Maintaining a keto lifestyle long-term requires more than just following low-carb recipes; it's about establishing habits that support your overall well-being. Here's how to build and sustain a keto lifestyle:

Develop a Balanced Meal Plan: Ensure your meal plan includes a variety of keto-friendly foods to avoid monotony and nutrient gaps. Incorporate healthy fats, moderate protein, and low-carb vegetables.

Be Consistent: Consistency is crucial for long-term success. Establish a routine that includes meal planning, regular exercise, and mindful eating.

Stay Informed: Keep up-to-date with keto-friendly foods and new nutrition research. This knowledge will help you make informed decisions that align with your health goals.

Tips for Sustainability

1. **Meal Prep:** Prepare meals and snacks in advance to avoid the temptation of high-carb options.
2. **Try New Recipes:** Keep your diet exciting by experimenting with new keto recipes and adapting ingredients to your taste.
3. **Join a Community:** Connect with others who are also on a keto journey. Sharing experiences and advice can provide support and motivation.

Continuing Your Weight Loss Journey

The keto diet can be effective for weight loss, but sustaining your progress requires ongoing effort. Focus on setting realistic goals and tracking your progress to remain motivated.

Tips for Continued Success:
1. Set Realistic Goals: Break down your long-term goals into smaller, achievable milestones. Celebrate each success to stay motivated.
2. Track Your Progress: Use a food journal or tracking app to monitor your meals and progress. This can help identify patterns and necessary adjustments.
3. Be Flexible: If you encounter a plateau or challenges, be prepared to adjust your diet or exercise routine to keep making progress.

Healthy Habits for Long-Term Success

Maintaining a healthy lifestyle extends beyond diet. Incorporate these habits into your daily routine to support overall health and long-term success:

- **Prioritize Rest:** Ensure you get quality sleep each night. Adequate rest is vital for recovery, hormone regulation, and overall wellness.

- **Manage Stress:** Employ stress-management techniques such as meditation, yoga, or deep-breathing exercises. Chronic stress can impact your health and weight loss efforts.

- **Stay Active:** Make regular physical activity a part of your routine by choosing activities you enjoy, such as walking, swimming, or strength training. This will help you stay active and healthy in a sustainable way. Excitingly, we've included a special 7-day keto-friendly exercise plan designed just for you in the bonus chapter!

Tips for Long-Term Health

1. Establish a Routine: Develop daily habits that support your health, such as regular exercise, balanced meals, and relaxation techniques.

2. Seek Professional Guidance: Consult with a healthcare provider or nutritionist if you need personalized advice or support.

3. Practice Flexibility: Allow for occasional indulgences while staying focused on your overall goals. Balance is crucial for a sustainable and enjoyable lifestyle.

Congratulations on reaching this milestone in your keto journey! Maintaining your results and embracing a keto lifestyle long-term requires commitment, but with the right strategies and mindset, you can achieve lasting success. As you celebrate your progress, stay focused on your health goals, and approach each day with a positive attitude, remember that physical activity plays a crucial role in complementing your dietary efforts. The next chapter is a bonus chapter featuring a 7-day keto-friendly exercise plan designed specifically for women. These effective exercises will help you amplify your results, boost your energy, and enhance your overall well-being. Your journey to optimal health is ongoing, and now you have the added tools of both nutrition and fitness to propel you forward. Stay motivated and embrace the benefits of a healthier, more vibrant life!

Bonus Chapter

7-Day Keto-Friendly Exercise Plan for Women

This 7-day exercise plan is tailored to support your Keto Egg Fast journey by promoting ketosis while strengthening your body, enhancing endurance, and improving overall health. These low-impact workouts are ideal for women at any fitness level. Remember to stay hydrated and listen to your body, as energy levels can fluctuate during ketosis.

Day 1: *Full-Body Low-Impact Strength Training*

Duration: 30 minutes

- **Warm-up:** 5 minutes (marching in place, arm circles, light stretching)
- **Circuit (3 rounds):**

1. Bodyweight Squats – 15 reps
2. Push-Ups (kneeling if needed) – 10 reps
3. Glute Bridges – 15 reps
4. Dumbbell Rows (light weights) – 10 reps per arm
5. Plank Hold – 30 seconds

- **Cool down:** 5 minutes (light stretches, deep breaths)

Day 2: *Cardio and Core Workout*

Duration: 25 minutes

- **Warm-up:** 5 minutes (jumping jacks, side steps, arm swings)
- **Circuit (3 rounds):**
1. Jump Rope or March in Place – 1 minute
2. Bicycle Crunches – 20 reps
3. Mountain Climbers – 20 reps
4. Russian Twists – 20 reps
5. Flutter Kicks – 30 seconds

- **Cool down:** 5 minutes (stretching, core-focused stretches)

Day 3: *Active Recovery and Stretching*

Duration: 20 minutes

- **Activity:** Light yoga or gentle stretching
1. Child's Pose – 2 minutes
2. Downward Dog – 1 minute
3. Cat-Cow Stretches – 10 reps
4. Seated Forward Fold – 2 minutes
5. Pigeon Pose (each side) – 1 minute each

- End with deep breathing and relaxation

Day 4: *Lower Body Strength Training*

Duration: 30 minutes

- **Warm-up:** 5 minutes (leg swings, lunges, hip rotations)
- **Circuit (3 rounds):**

1. Lunges (with or without weights) – 12 reps per leg
2. Step-Ups (on a chair or step) – 10 reps per leg
3. Sumo Squats – 15 reps
4. Wall Sits – 30 seconds
5. Calf Raises – 20 reps

- **Cool down:** 5 minutes (leg stretches, breathing exercises)

Day 5: *Cardio with Upper Body Focus*

Duration: 25 minutes

- **Warm-up:** 5 minutes (jumping jacks, arm swings, light jog)
- **Circuit (3 rounds):**
1. Jumping Jacks – 1 minute
2. Push-Ups – 10 reps
3. Tricep Dips (using a chair) – 12 reps
4. Dumbbell Shoulder Press – 12 reps
5. Plank with Shoulder Taps – 20 taps

- **Cool down:** 5 minutes (upper body stretches)

Day 6: *Core and Flexibility Routine*

Duration: 20 minutes

- **Warm-up:** 5 minutes (light stretching, side bends, hip circles)
- **Circuit (3 rounds):**
1. Plank Hold – 30 seconds
2. Side Plank (each side) – 20 seconds
3. Leg Raises – 15 reps
4. Bird-Dog – 10 reps per side
5. Seated Forward Bend – 1 minute

- **Cool down:** 5 minutes (core stretches, light yoga)

Day 7: *Active Rest with Walking*

Duration: 30-45 minutes

Activity: A brisk walk outdoors or on a treadmill
- Keep a steady pace, focusing on deep breathing

- End with a stretch, targeting any sore or tight areas

Success Tips:

- **Hydrate Well:** Drink enough water throughout the day, especially before and after workouts.
- **Focus on Recovery:** Give your body time to rest, and adjust the intensity of exercises if needed.
- **Modify as Needed:** If you feel fatigued while in ketosis, reduce workout intensity or duration.
- **Smart Nutrition:** Ensure you're fueling your body with protein-rich, egg-based meals for energy and muscle recovery.

This 7-day plan is designed to seamlessly integrate keto-based eating with effective workouts, helping you gradually build strength and endurance as your body adapts to ketosis.

Conclusion

Congratulations on finishing *The Keto Egg Fast Diet Cookbook for Women*! You've taken a meaningful step towards adopting a keto lifestyle with a focus on the egg fast. As you close this book, it's important to reflect on your achievements and look forward with assurance.

Celebrating Your Success

First and foremost, celebrate your progress. By embracing the egg fast and incorporating these egg-centric recipes, you've made significant advances toward improving your health and achieving your wellness goals. Each meal you've prepared and each hurdle you've overcome deserves to be recognized. Success is not just about reaching the final goal but also about the journey and effort involved.

Staying Committed to Your Health Goals

To sustain the benefits of your keto lifestyle and the egg fast, ongoing dedication is key. Keep your health goals in view by consistently applying what you've learned in your daily life. Whether it's adhering to keto principles, trying new recipes, or refining your meal plans, maintain your motivation and commitment. The habits you've formed during the egg fast will support your long-term health.

Final Words of Encouragement

As you continue, remember that every journey has its challenges. View these challenges as chances for growth and stay resilient. Use the tips and strategies from this book to overcome any difficulties you may encounter. Your dedication to your health is impressive, and with the knowledge and resources you now have, you're well-prepared to thrive on your keto journey.

Tips for Long-Term Success

1. Stay Updated: Keep informed about the latest keto research and trends to enhance your diet and adapt as necessary.

2. Plan Ahead: Regular meal planning will help you stay on track and make your keto journey more manageable.

3. Try New Recipes: Keep your meals exciting by experimenting with and creating new egg-based dishes.

4. Listen to Your Body: Monitor how different foods affect you and adjust your diet to meet your individual needs.

5. Find Support: Join keto communities or support groups to share experiences, gain motivation, and receive encouragement.

In summary, thank you for using this cookbook as your guide on the keto egg fast. May the success you've achieved inspire you to continue leading a healthier, more vibrant life. Your commitment is the cornerstone of your ongoing success, and you have all the tools necessary to make your keto journey both enjoyable and fulfilling. Here's to your continued health and success—cheers to what lies ahead!

Made in the USA
Las Vegas, NV
22 December 2024

15145837R00075